Dear Parents,

Is your child a new reader? If yes, one good way to help your child build confidence and word recognition skills is by introducing word families.

The die-cuts at the bottoms of the pages draw attention to three different word families (letters show through each die-cut shape).

Once your child can read "**ack**", then he or she can focus on the beginning letters and sounds:

> s**ack**, j**ack** qu**ack**

After the single words are learned, the pictures help your child read the words in phrases:

> **quack shack**   **quack on a sack**
> **shack on a jack**   **shack on a jack**

It's much easier to learn a group of words than to memorize them by sight one word at a time. A sight vocabulary is limited by the number of words that can be held in memory.

Recognizing words by families hugely increases the number of words that your child can know. It gives your child a way to sound out new words (reading specialists call these "word attack" skills), thereby increasing the likelihood he or she will feel successful.

Help your child with the 25 new words in this book by giving him or her multiple chances to read it until all the words are mastered.

Most important, have fun together!

Harriet Ziefert, M.A.
Language Arts/Reading Specialist

Quack Shack

by **Harriet Ziefert**

Illustrated by **Yukiko Kido**

flip-a

WORD

Word Families

The world is full of print. Written words are everywhere. It's impossible to learn printed words by memorizing them word, by word, by word. To make learning easier, words can be grouped into families.

The words in a word family have two or more letters that are the same. We read "ack" words and "ick" words, "eet" words and "ock" words. If you know "ack," then it's easier to learn quack, shack, and jack.

This book has words from three different word families. All the words in a family rhyme—which means you can add other words to the group by changing the first letter.

It's okay if some of the words you think of are not *real* words. If you make "nack" or "vack" or "zack," it's not wrong— as long as you know the difference between a real word and a nonsense word.

Flip each page and presto-change-o— a new word appears!

The
ack
Family

s h

sack

quack shack

sack on a jack

quacks with sack

shack on a jack

The ick Family

f
l
w
m
g
n
b
r
d
w
t

sick

sick chick

chick licks

chick kicks

sick chick licks

The

ock

Family

f
l
w
m
g
n
b
r
d
w
t

b l

sock

locks rock

socks rock

socks on a lock

block on a sock

The ack Family

back	crack
jack	pack
quack	sack
shack	snack

The ick Family

brick	chick
kick	lick
pick	quick
sick	stick

The ock Family

block	clock
dock	flock
knock	lock
rock	sock

Find the words in each family.

sock snack shack kick stick knock pick dock clock knock sack brick stick block chick pack lock rock sick quick lick flock quack brick jack lock sack clock block back sick kick crack lick dock chick sack quack back sock rock pick shack

Word Family Activities

- Choose two words from the word family and make your own "flip-a-word" illustrations. Remember to make a cut-out at the bottom of the page where the word family shows through.

- Words in a word family rhyme. Learn a song or a poem that rhymes and share it. Or read a book that rhymes and guess which words rhyme.

- Write or tell or draw a story using two or three of the characters in this book. What happens next?